5.00

Curtains up

The stage is black.

LIGHTS ON 2 SECONDS

CENTRE STAGE:

A man is sitting on the floor
he looks exactly like you
his legs are trapped in a giant mousetrap
he is talking but you can't hear him
unless you are a pig.

BLACKOUT 2 SECONDS

Consider the pig.

LIGHTS ON

Behind the man talking pig-talk
who is trapped in the mouse trap
we see a mother
her face is identical to your own mother's
she is nailed onto a cross
she is singing but you won't join in with her song
you don't want to take her down
and you won't want to dance with her
unless you are a wasp.

BLACK OUT 2 SECONDS

Consider the wasp.

LIGHTS ON
The music starts to build, slowly at first
pains net is falling gradually
a baby is laughing
exactly like your sister laughs
a claw is scraping across the ground towards you
the orchestra is way out of tune.

ENTER AT DAWN: THE QUEEN BEE AND ALL HER DRONES

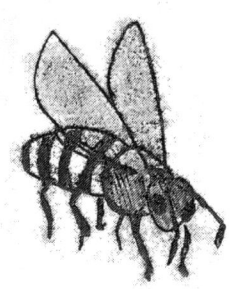

HOUSE of BEES
STEPHEN MURRAY

salmonpoetry

Artwork by Roisin Coyle
www.roisincoyle.com

Published in 2011 by
Salmon Poetry
Cliffs of Moher, County Clare, Ireland
Website: www.salmonpoetry.com
Email: info@salmonpoetry.com

Copyright © Stephen Murray, 2011

ISBN 978-1-907056-71-0

All rights reserved. No part of this publication may be reproduced or transmitted in any form or by any means, electronic or mechanical, including photography, recording, or any information storage or retrieval system, without permission in writing from the publisher. The book is sold subject to the condition that it shall not, by way of trade or otherwise, be lent, resold or otherwise circulated without the publisher's prior consent in any form of binding or cover other than that in which it is published and without a similar condition, including this condition, being imposed on the subsequent purchaser.

TYPESETTING: Siobhán Hutson

Salmon Poetry receives financial support from The Arts Council

> "It's a puzzle: each piece, each room, each time you put your hand to the knob, your mouth to the hand, your ear to the wound that whispers."
>
> RICHARD SIKEN

Acknowledgements

Thanks are due to the editors of the following journals in which some of these poems have previously appeared:

Cartier Street Review, Poetry Bay, Ropes, The Argotist. "Little Miss Infinity" originally used for "Number 9" exhibition with Roisin Coyle for Tulca 2006. Also "Visions of the Divine on Hare Island" for "Seconds Out" as part of Cúirt 2008 with Roisin Coyle.

Special thanks also to Jessie Lendennie, Dani Gill, Michèle Vassal, Dylan Harris, Kevin Higgins, Susan Millar DuMars and Over the Edge, Seán and Brighid Bán Breathnach, Brian Phelan, Andrew Byrne, Andrew Hassett, Alan Sheehan, Kieran Calvert, Elaine Feeney, Brendan Murphy, Mags Treanor, Daithi Magner, Dylan Harris, Éilís Ní Dhuibhne, my friends and families, Murray, Geraghty and Louki, and especially to Ronan Considine.

Contents

The Nail	13
Footprints	14
Memoirs of Woman's Aid	16
The Looking Glass	18
Childhood	19
Oh my, Oh my!	20
Son of a Goat... Part 1	21
Starling	23
House of Bees	24
Cacophony	26
Tammy: Love in a Children's Home	27
Chrysalis	29
Ice Wind Dale	30
Solvent Abuse	32
Prodigal Son	33
Adagio for Screams	35
February 22nd 1992: 06.15 AM: M25 Junction near Leatherhead	37
Chronic Anxiety Jazz Solo – No. 1	39
The Death of a She-Wolf	41
Ground Floor Garden Flat	43
Shape-shifter	44
Sleepy	45
Little Miss Infinity	46
Jody	48
Chronic Anxiety Jazz Solo – No 2	49
Naked	51
Coven of the Scarecrow	52
Bootleg Generation	55

Slumber	57
The Drone That Got Away	58
Son of a Goat... Part 2	59
An English Rose	61
The Reason	62
Wallpaper	64
Chronic Anxiety Jazz Solo – No. 3	67
Naked in Vienna	69
Galway Last Night	71
Sexy	73
South London Upon Corrib	75
An Ode to Barna, Co. Galway	76
Her Bloody Chamber	78
Son of a Goat... Part 3	79
The Demon	81
Visions of the Divine on Hare Island	82
Cigar in Mouth	83
Tammy on the Footbridge	84
A Letter to Prague	85
A Love Letter for The Queen of Wasps	86
Techno	88
The Bottle in the Cupboard	89
A Christmas Poem for A	91
An Irish Thing	92
Chronic Anxiety Jazz Solo No 4	93
Drone's Requiem	95
About the Author	97

for Koula

The Nail

The nail that gave way at the top
silenced the sound of the drop
as all hell hit the ground.

And a hurricane came
with an apron and mop.

It rained and it rained
and it never
did stop.

Footprints

In 1974 her footprints grew heavier by the swelling month.
Sank deep into sodden clay; bore the stamp of Dutch clogs.

Each footprint a scar in the muck.
Each laboured step a cave drawing of screaming calves
burning thighs and a groaning spine.

There were other footprints, those of a man
the mark of which, was of one who walks on the balls of his feet
like someone looking for something that he left on the ground
swerving from left to right.

By the end of that year her footprints lightened
bore the stamp of bare feet,
of one who had just discovered music, God,
then learnt to dance and pray.
Each footprint profound
a golden memory in the sods of the earth
each feathered step a cherished glimpse
of the secrets of the world.

There were other footprints also
an infant's in tiny sandals quick, light and short in step
as hers resumed their clog shape
grew heavier over barbed time
those footprints that stared at the ground seemed to stomp
hers backed off, seemed to fall to the ground and get back up
then fall to the ground and get back up.

When the second set of tiny prints appeared aside of hers
the first infant's grew larger that of a boy
the second that of a girl grew with his
and the prints that stomped and stared at the ground
vanished into a concrete city
where footsteps leave no mark.

As those little footprints grew larger hers changed shape
staying one step ahead of the fashion
developed a stagger and a stomp of their own
swerving from left to right constantly
wandered helplessly into deserts
where those two tiny prints wandered off on their own
seemed to fall to the ground then get back up
then fall to the ground and get back up.

Memoirs of Woman's Aid

Most of all, I remember being lost yet unafraid
in fields of cereal wheat.
I remember my grandmother's throne in the kitchen,
both kettle and cooker within arms reach
her freshly cooked bread and slipper-clad feet.
My grandfather's shotgun, the smoke from his pipe
I remember running terrified to bed past the life-size statues
of Jesus and Mary twice my size
being followed to sleep by cold pious eyes
I remember little or nothing of Erin Pizzey
though I remember Anne Ashby quite well.

I remember my sister staking claim over my pram
sore legs screaming in the burning sun
Kildare by tractor, Cardiff beneath stage lights.
Walking amongst giants at the Welsh National Opera,
my Auntie Sheila's egg-in-a-cup.
I remember screaming at the clown
with his bucket full of everything you'd never need
and nothing that you would, at Billy Smart's Christmas Circus.
I remember being six-years-old for the very first time
and what a great day that was,
picking my nose was something new
and there were tiger cubs at Dublin Zoo
but I remember little or nothing of the Chiswick High Road.

I remember the white Christmas in Adelaide Road.
My police bike with its blue siren lights that flashed for one day
and I remember the children divorce courts refused
invincible, brazen and highly amused by our accents.
I remember my father-upon-Thames
dashing, drunken and charming to boot
flashing a smile as he waved us good bye
on the red London Bus for the very last time.

I remember it all, in super 8 vision,
my very first book and my father's last look.
I remember little or nothing of the rat that shared a cradle
with my baby sister, suckling on her bottle as she slept
in the derelict Palm Court Hotel where we sheltered
with the battered wives of Erin Pizzey's Woman's Aid.

The Looking Glass

The Lion, the Scarecrow, and the Tin Man
have Dorothy pinned to the ground.
They scratch her and poke her
and pull at her hair and they dare her
to utter a sound.

Hansel is leading his sister
from the prison where both were released.
From the cottage of cake
to a chapel of hate
and the Wicked Wolf dressed as a priest.

The Mad Hatter is threatening Alice
as he lifts up her skirt passed her knees.
He brings her dead flowers
then rapes her for hours
amongst the old sycamore trees.

Prince Charming is dying skewered upon thorns
in satin robes bloodied and soaked
and the last thing he hears
beneath chandelier tears
are her screams from beyond the white oaks

A hooded red cloak lies discarded
and Tinkerbell is dressed as a witch
black petals descend
at the fairy tale's end
when a trusted friend makes her his bitch.

Childhood

Well done little man it's another charade
that you've caused as you sit by your bed-barricade
in your room
blowing the cigarette fume
into rings for the bruises
and mental abuse,
it's when mother goes mad
and empties the bottle that substitute dad
swears that he'll throttle your neck
you were late back from school
and your room is a wreck
and you know the number one rule:
don't step out of line
and always keep time.

But you're clumsy and you're of little use.
You're just like your dad you deserve the abuse.
Just like your parents deserve the excuse to the neighbour
the preacher and the schoolteacher.

It really was nothing at all.
I just bumped into wall
after wall, after wall.

And that's only fair, as well you know
for the tantrum you threw
at your substitute dad was too bad
now you hear a thunderstorm brew outside
you've got nowhere to hide, contemplate suicide.

While mother goes martini-mad
at the door the immediate future
looks bad from the floor
you ask yourself why
heaven's empty above
you're abandoned by love

and abandoned by God

Oh my, Oh my!

Oh my oh my
A crimson sky
A baby eating nettle pie
A broken wish
A shattered dish
The juice of twenty rotten fish
An eel beneath
A dying reef
A wind that blows
on broken teeth
Streaming tears
And children's fears
the blood that trickles
From the ears
The flies that feast
On dying young
Salt water in
the drowning lung
The final breath
The shores of Lethe
Sorrow and the
Pain of death
Oh my! Oh my!
The children cry
A murder for
A wicked lie.

Son of a Goat... Part 1

Yes, the house fell down
a woman screamed.

Mother I think.

Pictures fell off the wall, pipes burst
upstairs in the bathroom
the stand alone bath
the one with brass lion legs
bubbled like a cauldron
cracked-clean-in-two
someone called for help

it was Mother again I think.

Anyway, the water, boiling it was
crashed through the floor
ceramic tiles shattered
plaster on the walls and ceilings cracked
then the roof fell in.
"Shut the fuck up," a voice said

Mother again I think

but I hadn't said anything
honest.

Yes, if you must know
I was afraid, I was terrified
clutched teddy teardrop-tight
he had never been the same
since someone burnt out
his little plastic beady-bear eyes

Mother again I think.

Moving on, I ran
as fast a little legs can carry
the coffins of the parents
who they themselves buried alive
before they were born
forget I said that
it's finished, over, done with
scratch it, scrub it, rub it out
lets play truth or dare.

Starling

Starling
you have
you have been
the darling of the wood
for far too long.

You have
neglected
your nest
and the magpies
are eating
your children.

House of Bees

Dinner is at five, always at five
that is when the new drones come.

No one questions Herself
whose wings are the whole wide world.

We are spring-loaded rat-trap workers
poised to sting the hand that feeds.

We are beyond pest control.
Her Majesty's children.

Her song is the purr of the traffic outside
and her eyes are the blacked-out windows of cars.

Hyper-vigilant is that what society calls us?
What is wrong with that?

No one breathes a word
no one tells and no one wilts.

Danny arrived at five today
his eyes twitched from left to right.

No one batted an eyelid
and no one asked him why.

He will snap within the next three days
we all cracked-in-two within three.

Why are they staring at me he howls
and who scrubbed out their faces?

He thrashes at the world
fists and open palms swat the flashbacks.

Go now dear Danny, go to your Queen
she wants only to love you.

Like no one else will, she will love you
with solvents and sew up your eyes.

So go quick for winter is coming
and when your face is scrubbed out

they won't see you cry and in the drone
they won't hear you screaming.

Cacophony

The curtain is drawn
the stage alive with the ghosts of the lost
speaking fluent gibberish into turnip microphones
to an audience of tearful green metallic flies
and the rapturous applause of china dolls
dressed in Victorian dreams.
Today was the day the chandeliers came crashing to the floor.
The organist died mid-song falling face-flat-down
onto one final eternal terminal chord
bleeding from the ears and from the eyes.
It will hit you tonight while you sleep
when you wake weeping uncontrollably
in what will be your final and greatest performance ever.
For tonight is the night the puppets perform
without strings or storyline.
The band shall play in motionless silence
to an entourage of raggy dolls who sit
violently still with their eyes torn out.
While clowns turn childish laughter
into psycho screams in the silence
but for children's dreams
the tales to old folk fairies tell
senile on the carousel of muffled whispers
from the Jack in the box
that reveal a dark and terrifying secret
that is a secret no more.
The puppeteer is dead.
The puppeteer has always been dead.
Remember well your last night's decent sleep
It will have been your last.

Tammy: Love in a Children's Home

Tammy came to my room in the night in her slip, she was braless and brainless and breathless and only thirteen. She would sit at the end of my bed and part her legs ever so slightly. And my heart would beat a good thump of it, as her nipples pressed hard against soft white cotton. And her flesh was an evil genius, and her flesh was a criminal mastermind, and her flesh was Moriarty.

Oh Tammy, oh Tammy trembled the dust *burn me, burn me, burn me.*

Then she spoke about men and the back seats of cars as she opened my window and unclipped the stars. I drooled at the mouth for the marmalade of her and I longed for the skin of her butterscotch thighs. I would give her the world, the land and the sea, and then for the salt of her sweat I would throw in the skies. And her lips were the fall of mankind and her blue eyes were time spent in jail.

Tamara, Tamara grovelled the night *rev up the engines and fire out the lights, I am yours.*

And her scent was a Jedi mind trick and her innocence was an old man's tongue.

Tammy fucked every man on our street
and came to my room in the night in her slip to torment me.
They fucked her behind bushes and they beat her black in
    blue daylight.
She seemed to enjoy the drama of it. I think it made Tammy feel grown up.

And her voice was a song and her skin was a life sentence.

Tamara, Tamara God damn you to the gutters screamed the bright white light of the day as her teenage spaceship crashed somewhere in the silhouetted distance.

Tammy came to my room in the night in her slip to torment me.
With the flesh of her thighs and her bright blue eyes,
and I pandered to the dust and took great gulps of the thin
    air she breathed.
Oh for one crumb of her naval. Oh for one spoonful of marmalade.
Oh for young Tammy who was only thirteen with a body to cry for
and a face that would launch a thousand fists.
Tammy came to my room in the night in her slip,
she was braless, and breathless, and brainless, and only thirteen.

Chrysalis

Leaps from auburn, butterscotch childhoods, a metamorphosis
from the cherry blossom, autumn breeze to shimmering
patterns of ripe flesh traced by fresh fingertips.

Tongues twist, saliva convalescent dresses wounds from
cruel thorns, skewers bulging loins and rips the petals
of an untouched rose; tears the lamb to shreds.

Claustrophobic dreams asphyxiate silence,
throttles flesh-filled-space where naked bodies
spit acid into the eyes, brittle membranes burst.

Shapes shift in motionless darkness, hot breath of petal-sweat,
bodily fluids photosynthesizing unblemished skin; a hormonal orchestra
to beat to death the silence with a battered brass lipless horn.

Conscience-cradled secrets disembowel discovery, the atavist spreads
once crumpled wings, flies guilt-blind into a shadow-clad statue
    of Our Lady,
a dozen Our Fathers, a thousand Hail Mary's, a swirl of flesh.

Ice Wind Dale
for Louise Mucha

At the sides of the road
where the rime white trees
in the ice wind dale
shrink into a memory
on a rook-black night
with the sound sucked out
and the last fire doused
fumbling in the darkness
for a warm safe house
when the snow turns red
as the stag falls dead
there's a subtle urgent stirring
in a crooked man's bed
and his hands feel cold
as his breath pumps fast
there's a smell of something wicked
that has long-since passed.

As her mid-stride stiffens
in the scythe-cold dark
there's a shuffle in the bushes
in the wind gripped
skin-stripped ice wind dale
there's a sleet-pierced cry
the weeping of a father
and a mother-plucked dry
from the cage-close gloom
springs a cut throat moon
smiling like a jackal with
its teeth knocked out
where the child drops smiles
as the sky spills stars upon
the rime white trees

and the long skilful fingers
of the crooked man's wiles
creep upon her cheek like
a corpse-cold breeze.

There's a fissure in the ice
of the skate-steel lake
the sun rises like a sentry
with secrets primed to bake
inside a stone-built kiln
upon the guilt-hushed ice
beside the rime white trees
where the wind thinks twice
beneath the sole-crushed snow
in the devastated soil
where the mandrakes grow
there's a trail that disappears
behind a veil of light
where a crooked man takes office
with interfering fingers
wearing cardinal-white
and the ice wind dale
reveals a fear-plucked goose
with it's bones picked dry
as all hell breaks loose
in the valley wearing daylight
like a hangman's noose.

.

Solvent Abuse

Our brains on dry ice

        pupils full as black moons

        buzzing around loveless corridors

A hundred wing-beats

        per tiny frozen second

        multi-coloured in the silver world

Floating at the speed of cartwheels

        bouncing slowly off each other

        like balloons at a birthday party

for a child in a wheelchair.

Prodigal Son

On the day I came back there was thunder
and the sun left its scar in the hay

there sat my sister in love with the wire
that strangled the light from the day.

All the shopkeepers came out to greet me
their daughters stood proud by the sides

I would flash them a grin with the flail of my skin
then recoil like the ocean-whipped tide.

There stood there a man like my father
who sparkled like new-polished glass

and his words bore the feathers of eagles
as he tripped like a broken-hoofed ass.

When the ice cream van-man came playing his tune
his children I knew all their names.

He swapped me his young for a cancerous lung
as I slew the black dragon of change

For my father I'd sample each whisky
for my sister I'd throw back a beer

then I'd roll me a joint of my secrets
which I'd spit into some stranger's ear.

For my mother I lit me a cigarette
which I put out in the palm of my hand

for her love was as true as what razorblades rue
and a heart is a handful of sand.

Then at once I wept for her beauty
then I screamed for the lack of it all.

For she was the song on the stairwell
where the wallpaper's torn from wall.

Adagio for Screams

I remember you well sipping twelve-year-old single malt battle juice
flashing that bullet-proof smile at armour-plated dolly birds
who'd impale themselves upon your past then disappear
in broken high heels dismantled by your high ideals
the moth-god of butterflies, our rogue prince of Sixmilebridge.

Till that bullet-proof smile shattered somewhere between joy and terror
when she walked in with Mozart all breath-taking femininity
and delicate sensibilities to opened you up like a clam
before the burning sun to let your ghosts back in.

The infant who crawled naked through the gates of hell and came
    out singing.
The last time I saw you, you were dragging your forgotten footsteps
with your head bowed to your demons amongst limping pigeons
    in the techno rain, muttering to yourself beneath the weeping
    grey stony walls of the Crescent Memorial.

You were locked in some place where you are twelve again and your
Mother stands dressed to the nines on the Dock Road
pimping your ten-year-old brother, dressed as a girl
to men made of whispers and spit.

Because she walked out on you with Barber and Beethoven arm-in-arm.
And she left you nothing but the cake that she had baked for you
filled with your father's old razor blades to lacerate your silver tongue.

I remember you well trawling the beds of strangers for crumbs
    of affection.
To feed the insatiable hunger of absolute failure.
Your bloodied hand still marks the wall Sir, where you stumbled in drunk
having beaten a stranger half to death for looking sideways at your ghosts.

In your padded cell of broken glass where wolves blew down your
    house of cards.
I remember you well, shattered and foetal on a crack-den settee
with your hands buried in your crotch and all your friends
    on suicide watch.

Now you wander barefoot through asylum corridors
where little boys run around in corsets

Howling your insect agony in the iron maiden of your dreams

A requiem for an unspoiled youth

An adagio for screams

February 22nd 1992: 06.15 AM: M25 Junction near Leatherhead

Sirens flash tumblers turn
Greeks wail women kneel
Arms embrace tears fall
Words weep triggers switch
Numbers dial voices crack
Sisters crumble wind sobs
Mothers scream clouds lament
Men cry tongues choke
Cameras flash papers print
Hearses roll shovels dig
Darkness moans grief wakes
Ghosts haunt Gods hide
Fingers link shoulders mourn
Smiles drown angels murder
People love touch comforts
Metal cuts skulls crush
Skin breaks lungs burst
Candles melt breaths disperse
Flowers wither buildings fall
Children stumble beloved die
Legs buckle lips kiss
Cars crash knees graze
Love blossoms hands hold
Memories fade storms howl
Heads bow eyes close
Morgues chill incense burns
Psalms pray hymns sing
People live corpses rot
Coffins close, eventually
But death does not compute

His mother bought him
An around the world airline ticket
For his eighteenth birthday that day
The papers printed their ages and names in black

Andrew 18, Mark, 18, Liberty 17, Daniel 17, James 19

Like gospel verses

We lit all eighteen candles anyway

But none for us had the appetite for cake, nor the breath, or the will to blow out a single one of those tiny flawless flames.

Chronic Anxiety Jazz Solo – No. 1
for Dave

When time was a tear that dripped from black-space-skinned a victim of things that had passed not (yet before) the martyrdom reasons and the sky lay odds with each other God hung on a telephone that never rang with His voice like a thousand quarrelling stars (His was that) face of a corpse you wanted to fuck, embalming mascara incense in a cold room (contemplation) when the wind was a conspiracy theory and cartoon Jews spun gold from (hay when skin) fizzed goosebumps were the footprints of sin that sat in a nail-sack love-lodged dirty in the back of your throat in the gut-pit like a widow at the wedding of the first-blood-breath and the last-rasped-cough bore witness to winters passed, ricochets voiced in silence's echo-shell

in the Chapel of the Sisters of Unrelenting (Shame hung us) by wrist-cold-chains in chambers pregnant with penance (the unplayable bore) us to ignominy's cruel and toothless midwife, raw wailing stubs of fingers with new-born gums burst through placenta's nauseating womb-filth fell on cold ceramic tiles and were crushed beneath whose boot I do not know...

Eyes front, breathe, calm.

A window, a garden, the world, the sky, nice folk at regular chores, a sunflower

It seems to sing

Soprano on Omaha Beach

and is withered oncely by a wind-raped tirade of acid rain that bent you over and funked you backwards again mister for no apparent reason saw you coming, (quite frankly) played you like a tin whistle to the tune of a flute in the key of puberty's disjuncture and a voice torn-off rip-roared both balls dropped heavy as billiards in old men's socks and cocks swung in blue vein school showers segued into dragons' tongues (dripping-(fuck)-off) and curses crazy declarations spat at Christ by children with metal hands and digital lips puking ones and naughts flashing siren's (honesty before love)'s strobe-stripped and left us naked where we stand in awe of things that bounce off walls made religion up on the spot-spare-space and throttled possibility for every thought that goes in between when in the playground all at once ignorance's brittle membrane burst evolution's hymen breached-bled till not-quite-dead snapped shut twicely and the only word we might ever want to hear again is

'Bingo'

ringing our name

— Your name Sir?

Mister, how long has it been since you last took piss?

The Death of a She-Wolf

I came to her house
in the glade of dead trees
and her lair was a den in the muck
her silence a belly of moments split open
in seconds made bad
in a heartbeat gone out
that was cleaved all at once into two
into four into eight into sixteen
stillborn litters of mutes
and her pelt was a mess
and her throat was a stinking tomorrow
in the night made of fangs
in an abscess of things freshly skinned
the steam of her blood
was the purge of thin air
that sang to the streams
of things we would all one day forget
For a she-wolf is dead
and a mongrel remains
with her tongue full of stings
where a grovelling whine
not a howl nor fresh scatter
of feathers for the meal of a fowl
and a bag of dead bones
for the tiny crushed skulls of her pups
made of panting and yelps
beneath boots blind as bats
that have squandered youth's invincible rhyme
for all the silence that ferrymen barter for time
and for butchers who whisper
to dead raw meat in their way
On the day she found God
he was skinning the sky
he was dressed as a jester
having buried the moon
in the shit of a hunter's guilt
and he muttered in tongues

to pigeons and rats
he has made her of mince
and shall feed her to cats
when the sword-song and sparrow
extinguished the saints
so out went her stare
like a Christmas begot

and her tears were the loot of the snow
as her tracks disappeared in the thaw
and oh for give us the detonating robin's red heart
for the predator's thirst cull-clipped to the claw
for a she-wolf is dead
and her litter is thrown
to the mouth of the day
and the cry of decay gets louder
by the stinking minute
in her gob made of gums without teeth
and oh for the rivers can sing
we are full of dead fish
we are as cold as an eel song
we are all that that is left
save the stench of her breath

Who put out her shadow?
Who silenced the growl?
Who stitched up dead space
with the beak of a chicken?
It was the chattering insects
or a head without eyes
it was the dribbling lunatics
who have played out their time
on the strings of her harp
that is fashioned in bone and despair
we are fashioned in bone and despair

for a she-wolf is dead
and her pelt is a mess
and her howl is the end of thin air
thin air, and her howl is the end of thin air.

Ground Floor Garden Flat

In her ground floor, garden flat in the South
where she told me that music and Jesus were dead
as she sat turned away at the end of the bed.

She told me the 'it' crowd, the coke-snorting shit crowd
were like horsemen of the apocalypse.

And that women were liars to test man's desire
and the vagrant who begged on the street was messiah.

I believed every single word that she said
as she watched me through eyes in the back of her head.

Then she turned towards me and she threw me a grin
that said take me to bed for an evening of sin.

In her ground floor, garden flat in the South
where I saw a spider crawl out of her mouth.

She pretended she hadn't notice me notice
and I fell in love as she smiled beneath eyes that were
yearning to weep

in a ground floor, garden flat in the South
with a girl who ate spiders and spoke in her sleep.

Shape-shifter
for Anastasia

She perches, seraph-like, staring
into an infinity of nothingness
in a cemetery for the not-quite-dead.

Her image snags in the corner of my eye
like the first gentle sigh of summer that
carries the scent of fresh flowers upon a grave.

Her beauty, claustrophobic, violent, her spirit
unquenchable, her myriad dreams sprawl
before me like invincible children playing dead at my heels.

She beckons me to drink from her serrated chalice
to share her menagerie of deformity and genius
to indulge in the alchemy of her skin as we exhaust ourselves
playing matador to the devil.

I watch her lips move as she talks with magical eyes
that dance as her words bounce of her thoughts
as she pulls the moon from her breast and wraps it
in the boundless darkness of her nonsensical tragedy.

Unbridling the silhouettes of the night she casts
her black petals of woe into the September sky
and garnishes the nebula with the glitter of a transient bliss.

Then her eyes close and she is lost
mumbling the passages of some clandestine prayer.

Dissolving into silence like a soul that draws the veil of death
where nightmares wait with baited breath.

In the terrifying still
tranquillity hangs on the hinges of her waking move.

She sleeps naked,

wearing the universe inside out.

Sleepy

I like to watch her sleep
To feel her breath collide in space with mine

To kiss her soft skin
 Like water lilies, cinnamon and cream;

The epitome of innocence
Her eyelids flicker in a dream

I marvel at her perfect creation
And I praise Gods work

"Thank you Lord
You have surpassed yourself."

Little Miss Infinity
for Roisin

Infinity was a mystery
though no one really knows
she was visited one winter
by a murder of sad crows.

They played for her a song
upon their black violins
with broken-hearted melodies
on rusty wire strings.

She nestled in their feathers
and she made their nest her home
but now they're gone
and Little Miss Infinity's alone.

She slumbers on their plumage
all alone at number nine
till one night she hears a music box
and the filthy snort of swine.

The bathroom tap is dripping
and the lights are all lit low
the cupboard door is banging
where the shadow bracken grow.

It happened while she slept one night
when she woke up to find
a boy who had four faces
and a clock that told no time.

Each face told her a story
both fantastical and wild
while shadows on the banisters
were creeping op the tiles.

Now she feeds her solitude
to the pigs beneath the bed
and the boy who has four faces tells
all the crows are dead.

And the carousel spins backwards
as the clowns move in
from the children catcher's circus
to her prison cell of skin.

She wanders in infinity
but her legs refuse to stand
she reaches into darkness
for an unclean hand.

In the black and swollen murkiness
she finds a friendly claw
and in the silent darkness
hears an old familiar craw.

"Look" says the crow "Infinity
let's see what we can find"
and there she sees infinity
a-waltzing in her mind.

So she gathers up some broken quills
and summons windy weather
she sails across the silver hills
on a carpet made of feather.

Now she's soaring above rooftops
and she sails above the crowds
against the snarling elements
above the cheering crowds.

And she sings to them
"that everything impossible is mine
for I am Little Miss Infinity
who lives at number 9."

Jody

Jody swears that Uncle Butterfly told her
says she spoke to him through buttercup-a-phones
that is how she knew what she knew
whereas we wouldn't have a clue.

It was the ladybirds what told her the secret.
The big one. Fact. Seriously. No shit.

It was the giant squid who was running things.
He was running the whole show.
He was dishing out orders to the dolphins
who met the Jews in secret locations
who in turn fed the television networks
and the CIA were in on it
as were Greenpeace and the Swiss.

Mind control, subliminal messages, hypnosis, propaganda.
The ladybirds had dirt on the lot of them
they had a ladybird working on the inside,
had them bugged.

They wrapped her in a blanket today
and took her off to live in a shivering cell.

She sees things clearer now.
Says that we are all blind.

Every. Single. Last. One. Of. Us.

Looking back I think she was right.
I can still see her standing naked in the moonlit bog
her eyes are closed and her hands are outstretched before her,
her fingers reading the braille of the stars.

Chronic Anxiety Jazz Solo – No 2
for Vade Nadrol

— Sir, your name Sir? You need to sleep Sir. How long has it
   been since you slept?

Days? Weeks? Who are these people?

— This is not a game Sir. Sir, your name please.

so the last die rolls on this monopoly board where we have hotels
(on every street (we own) us) we charge no rent and we get fucked out
since our inheritance was never bankable (you could not
bank on ((it) was) romance)
stretching out into the final shrivelling in a place without bus stops
sin and regret snapped at the scabs on our feet
love was a drum and a promise and God was a mescaline worm
in your heart screaming too many answers all at once and leaving
   you with none
they say you saw the face of God and found it made of madness

the flesh gone wrong when the heart was the canvas...

— Sir, look Sir, the walls they are breathing Sir.

the walls breathe...

when the canvas of time expressed itself with a rusty wire brush
hearts made of...

— Sir, how long has it been since you ate Sir? Since you ate.

...bright yellow syllables of our palates
echoes we jarred, subtitling our breakdowns
existence wanting to intellectually evolve but not at this speed not here
on Mount fucking Sinai with Jesus hanging on the cross bleeding

    the tears of women
and human conscience to remind of our sins
not in this place...

– Sir, I think there's somebody else in the apartment, Sir

– Sir, have a drink Sir, it will help you slow down

How long has it it been now since you pissed, slept, ate?

– Sir, your name Sir?

Naked

Naked she is the controller of all things.

As her lazy left hand rests carelessly
on the perfectly inward swing of her hip
the arcs of her breasts and nipples
that point at the sun.

The stopper of time and the changer of all things
when naked she is

the world spins on her axis.

Coven of the Scarecrow
for Rowan Somerville

Once upon a mountain where
the heartbeats of the bodhrán
bang a whispering of thunder
to the corpses in the ground

there rambled through a thicket
with her red hair in a locket
a man called Jack and Jill thought
he was quite the cut o' man.

She was sat upon a pile o' bones
feasting with the panthers
in the Coven of the Scarecrow
with the joker in her palm

and she dealt for him a hand of
cards and beckoned him to gamble
all he knew was set in stone against
the scriptures in the sand.

She held a flush and watched the
queen of clubs take him apart
then she fed him beetle grubs
to watch him vanish into darkness

and when he came to waking
how he felt the mountain shaking
for she held him in her arms
and then she sang to him at last.

She said that she'd been waiting
with the sinners and forsaken
and the wickens in the wood
gave her his likeness in a doll.

And she'd a filled it full of pins
if only hearts were made of metal
but he'd plucked her like a nettle
from her bed of poison thorns.

Then she led him through her siren's
door and let her garments fall and
she said "if my Lord, you'll be my King
then I shall be your whore."

And as they fell like death together
oh their shadows rose like hackles
so they growled all night like jackals
to the howling of the moon.

When morning came he rose like Christ
a throwing back his shoulders
he said "now my love I'll show you
where the lightning seeds are sewn.

We'll dance beneath the apple tree
and drive Saint Patrick back to sea
in the Coven of the Scarecrow
we shall live forever more.

We'll have ourselves an orgy
on the banks of the black Shannon
and upon the Hill of Tara
we shall build a shrine to Pan."

So they waged a hocus-pocus
against the flooding of the earth
then they swat a plague of locusts
with the smoke of burning turf.

Oh the harlequin was dancing
when they bet the Ace of Spades
against the King of Hearts who hadn't
won a soul in half an age.

As his Queen laid down her hymen
Jill bet the dawn against the stars
but Jack was King of Diamonds
and the King of Hearts the fool.

Said Jill "My love I can't stop
now for all the joy I've tasted
until this sober world is wasted
crawling naked on the floor

see I'll take back what Jesus takes
for Tara and for Ireland's sake
and then my love give birth to snakes
and then give birth to more.

And we won't see the virgin
shimmer through a shroud of lies
and we won't stop until we see
the whites of Pilate's eyes.

And they won't point their arrows
as their stone cathedrals fall
nor their guns where we stand naked
proud against the Pontiff's Wall.

So lead me through your chamber
door then take me on the stony
floor and I shall be your Goddess
and the dawn shall be your whore.

We shall feast beneath the apple tree
and drive Saint Patrick back to sea
in the Coven of the Scarecrow
we shall live forever more."

Bootleg Generation
for Killian Rogers

I will not be passionate about your washroom advertising campaign nor, will the hairs on the back of my neck stand on end as I fill out your Microsoft Excel spreadsheet.

I will not get butterflies in my belly when I wheel your wheelbarrows into a skip.

I will not put my heart into your filing cabinet or my soul in to your sales report.

I will not break into song when I answer your phones.

Adrenalin will not pump through my veins while I deliver your memos.

Your marketing communications literature, being neither art, sport or pornography means nothing to me.

I will not tremble with emotion at next week's team-building session.

The Holy Spirit will not descend upon me and grace me with anything resembling a religious experience as I stand at your assembly line.

I will not dance on the spot for your customers, they have never been right. Not once.

Tending your bar or waiting your tables does not give me a sense of achievement.

I will not be inspired by your in-staff training or thrilled by your companies increase or decrease in profits.

Being your employee of the month will not make me a better human being, a more accomplished lover, or decrease the size of my waistline.

Being punctual for work does nothing more than deprive me of sleep.

Wearing your company's uniform will never, ever make me proud.

I will not lie awake at night hoping you are happy with my work.

I will not be motivated by your encouragement, disheartened by your disappointment, or moved to tears by your company's fluctuating efficiency.

In short, I will do your fucking job, but, do not expect me, to care.

Slumber
for Aoife

You are my morning these days
pictured naked, half dreaming
soothed by a hymn of soft moans
eyes drinking subtle glimpses
of sunshine's scream for attention
hands caressing the lithe contours of
some lady-Christ unconscious self
a dreamy wedding cake
eaten whole alone
a celebration of slumber's
gentle rape.

The Drone That Got Away

A sincerely felt razor-blade of self given gladly to the moment.

        The drone that got away now made of light.

A sky designed by Gods made of colour.

        Sits by the shore and dreams of one who can
        love and sting without want or sacrifice.

The music that is whispered by stars, stops.

        Weeps for the heart of a wasp.
        Tears off his own wings.

The ocean holds its breath for the ebbing tide
hiccups hold the lung to ransom.

        And is carried away at last by shadows at Wit's
        End.

Son of a Goat... Part 2

Okay, so yes, it was raining
great big splinters of broken glass
punctured my tiny chicken thighs
my little red-boy-lips peeled back
tantrum's agony going ape-shit at it
son of a goat I was they said
and poor teddy with his burnt out eyes
whispered STOP too late
banged into a wall of night I did
it was a man six times the size of a six-year-olds world
put a black plastic bag over my head he did
bundled me into the boot of a car
heard a woman's voice laugh

Mother again I think

felt something shift beside me, above me, below me
squirming all around me, babies in black sacks
socks stuffed in their mouths
heard the car pull up beside running water
a man's heavy boots walked through rushes
then a voice

Mother again I think

told him to go and fetch the wicker baskets.

When I drifted ashore the music started
teddy and I parted ways
I pulled his arms and legs off
set fire to his polysynthetic filling told him to
shut the fuck up shut the fuck up shut the fuck up
the song that played I hated with an infernal passion
it was one of Mother's old favourites

Doctor Hook I think Doctor Hook I think Doctor Hook I think
kept running, kept raining, kept bumping into your man
Mister Wall of Famished Night
my little legs now thirty-three
hitched a ride on a rocking horse
heard voices in my head

Yep, Mother again I think.

Pulled plastic bags over my own skull, filled them with puke and tears
Felt needles in my arms, found a treasure hunt of little brown bottles
with my very own name on them that had been left for me by

Mother again.

An English Rose
for Lucy

Her song in time to my heartbeat
in tune to my every whim

she sings to me there
from the therapist's chair;

my rose in the garden of sin.

The Reason
for Michèle Vassal

There is a reason why men stand tall,
throw back their shoulders
push out their chests yet find themselves
at odds with the space around her.

It is the reason that poets exist,
the reason for which the word chivalry came to be.
It is why banners bearing her name
fly in the fluttering hearts of growling men.

It is the same reason jealous women
whisper behind their hands to each other
why strong men tear the meat
from the bones of boar with their teeth
driven mad by lust and wine.

It is why sunsets melt and horizons slip
off the delicate turn of her shoulders.
It is why anger crumbles
disarmed by her lip-bitten smile.

It is the first breath of war-torn wind
through fields of undiscovered jasmine.
It renders killers powerless
brings Gods crashing to their knees
commanded to obedience by her faintest of touch.

It is the unwitting blow to the solar plexus
of unassumingly breath-taking femininity.
It is the temperance of all things wild
the taming of the carnivore with subtle hand gestures;
the corruption of priests with naked laughter.

It is the flight of swans
and the stomping hoof of the bull.
It is the courting ritual of wild horses
and the song of the moon to dying stars.

It is the tracing of every contour of her face
with the faintest brush of an artist's eye.
The drinking of her words
with the inquisitive palate of Galileo.

It is the whisper of thunder to scorched sand
and the voice of the orphaned ghosts singing
a sweet hymn to end at last
the silent suffering of clowns.

Wallpaper

First a fairground
perfect colours and a carousel

the song that played
became your song

lips closed around candy floss

stepped off a rollercoaster
into a chapel

the sex was great.

Bought a house, semi-detached.

Wallpaper.

Six months and a moment
later.

Silence pregnant with a row.

Wallpaper

Ten years and a lifetime
on.

The long drive home
just around the corner.

From the job
that fucking job

the wife you hate
and the wallpaper

the mood swings

the screaming children

the his and hers
personality disorders

wallpaper

and the television

the broken washing machine

the stranger in your bed

wallpaper

and the sex

when she chooses

the job, the screaming kids

the car, the television

soap operas, chat shows

wallpaper

one day you'll tell her
one day you'll come screaming

clenching your fists, breathing fire
slinging faeces at the wall

the wallpaper
that fucking wallpaper

smashing glass
screaming children

she will cry
phone her mother

the kids will cower from you

a chat show host will point
a priest's finger at you

you will cut your feet
on the splinters of your vows

you will not be let forget
ever

they will remind you of it
over and over again

your humiliation will become
their next dramatic addiction

happiness shall haunt you
mock you where ever you look

the television
the sulking teenagers

soap operas, chat shows
prison food

sex

wallpaper.

Chronic Anxiety Jazz Solo – No. 3

Breath, concentrate on the flame, light, inhale, exhale.

Relax, smoke, have a drink

– Sir, I don't think we're alone Sir, there's someone else here Sir here in the house Sir

Has it been a week yet?

Daylight, churchgoing feet, requiem bells, it must be Sunday

hymns and screams for help and please much more than a whimper much less
than a scream put that in your ones and your noughts flank it with algebraic symbols
greater than and less than the sum of those you keep your secrets from give it cosines and go signs
and
stop signs multiply the bitch by pi then go take a mirror, use your yoga, your
breathing techniques your inner peace and go stick it up arse-wise in no uncertain terms.

– Slow down Sir you need to slow down. You are not yourself Sir.

Between the green man and the red in the land of the amber man and the barking dog
in the spider's hole each moment, a hooded shadow with a smokers claw that you will
not see till the cold scythe of your sins falls upon the back of your neck.

Don't throw them at me (those detonating disapproval looks) on your walk back home from church, save it for when you are beating your wife or choosing your daughters new leotard then the heart shall be the cage for your soul
and the only men who shall beat their chests shall be rapists at a vampires ballet.

And reasons for being, played themselves out, punctuated by mistakes and matters of the heart and moments were constellations of stars that would eventually die in a bog somewhere at the end of memory when god was music and hungry eyes and hearts prayed

for a teacher, a
father, a
reason.

– Sir, there is some one here to see you.

Naked in Vienna
for Mac

On the day we fell into that black place
where the peach sunset melted
like a golden tear, welling up
in the black eyelid of the Viennese horizon.

The bulrushes of the Danube
rose up like Nefertiti's eyelashes
the moon plucked a silver hare's head
from the black top-hat of the sky and we
prayed (for what it was worth) for time to stop
a while, and it did.

The sky (it seemed), had shed its veil and
paused a while to observe with us, the universe and
stars reflected in the water's surface
where we plunged our naked bodies
heart-first in.

I see those moments enshrined
flashed back in an instant, every time
I blink, the gentle waltz of our pale limbs
our laughter stripped naked of hesitant
thought, and the mantra of the mating calls
of frogs, crickets and creatures whose names
I hope I never know.

Each moment was a Galilean whore
to bathe our feet, a Goddess to bow to,
a lover to pine for on winter nights,
a mother to take us to her breast
and a friend to know us beyond
the boundaries of self.

It was love, (for what it was worth)
closing its warm arms around us
in the black depths of the Danube
beneath the light of dying stars
at the threshold of time itself.

Galway Last Night

2.45am, Sunday, Dominick Street

for Pat Bracken

They are pouring out from alternative, indie,
boiler rooms, abdomens bared, puking
into gutters; they are roaring for sound to
fill the silence of unfulfilled testicles.

They are screaming in high heels, staggering
awkwardly as hippos on stilts, they are lifting
their skirts and dropping their knickers,
squatting to piss behind glittering parked executive cars.

Fair play to them, sure, don't we only live once.

They are squashing into Costello's Kebab House
like maggots into the decomposing belly of a pigeon,
they are beached on street corners cheeks bloated chewing
slowly like feasting walrus's with coleslaw beards

And the streets are weeping piss, choking back vomit
into student dorms and filling out prescriptions for
the morning-after pill to flush away the trash that blows
like tumbleweed on Dominic St passed the Angels Club

Where Baltic midriffs snake around poles to sleeping
men with heads bowed dribbling into curried chips where seagulls
in balaclavas swoop with sawn-off beaks and the sun shines
    for scavengers
to clear away the remains of last night's lamb of God from side
    of the road

And 8am denies all knowledge once the street cleaners have
passed by in their fully-armoured sanitary cleansing tanks
like the secret police of the Pontiff sent to scrape the skin of
    the harlot city
with the regurgitating guts of the atavist and dump it into
    the forgetful sea

Sure isn't today Sunday, and confession a wonderful thing.

Sexy

The thing with Sexy was hard to spot
harder to put into words see, when Sexy
shed her youth and announced herself
to the wide-eyed world there was something
the world could never quite put its finger on
for want of a better expression see, the
thing with Sexy was never what she said
it was what she didn't say, the things she left
out that would bring thunder grovelling
at her doorstep and for that I loved her.

Not sure I can describe her and do justice
to either her, myself or the moments she
made, hand on hip, heart in mouth see
Sexy was a secret, maybe the greatest
secret of them all. A rocket that would
never lift off from the tip of her tongue and
let's not even go there when it comes to the
tip her tongue because that was a different ball
game altogether, ice hockey for angels
and if you didn't get it then it was your loss
find God, give up wheat and dairy
go online, find someone, see

It was what sexy didn't reveal that made
her so, wore a thong when single, panties for
the man she loved, (when convenient) we suspected she was
fluent in more than just the language
of hooded intent, that fireworks didn't belong
to her but we would grant her that and throw
in the dawn because no one deserved it more
see Sexy never hiked her skirt up too high
she had far too much respect for the sky
not to mention herself and one growling day
beneath the grovelling heavens Sexy walked in
to announce the secrets of the world.

See, Sexy had gotten herself a foot massage
from the moon three nights passed, shadows
stepped to one side as she crossed the threshold
of our world dressed in a veil of subtle
contours, stitched together by midnight
she held court and silence listened
as did we, she told us she would transcend
flesh and leave her body to the woodsman
and we watched the unassuming ballet
of her metamorphosis from icon to Goddess
the fabric of her blouse could no longer
silence the gospel of her nipples, the lightest
parting of her legs was like a hymn in Mecca
Sexy was pregnant and we (as was our privilege)
sang to the turning of the world.

South London Upon Corrib
for Tamsin

The night after she left
we watched the moon turn red
as the river roared her name
in fluent Corrib tongue
we heard her swirling syllables of sass
spiral clay-bound in pirouetting eddies
black as old man's stout.

Then the moon turned white
and we got twenty lashes
of a storm's tail wind-whipped in
from the Atlantic's watercolour palette
with a dark and angry brush
it was the shoes Tamsin
it was those shoes

Platform heels and vengeance-red
and it was that flip-top mirror
lipstick-watch and those chef slippers
and it was that girl beast
pluck-fucking our heart strings
flooring us with the lyrical flick
of her Crane-kick tongue

And it was the roar of her smile
like a flash of pink lightening
that commanded the Corrib to hush
then for the lunar eclipse
we blamed her lip-red shoes
for making the full moon blush.

An Ode to Barna, Co. Galway
for Jimmy Greaney and Tommy Gannon

They haunt this place like clockwork
In broken shoes and musty blazers
From the dignified noon to the gentle swerve
Of afternoons sat sipping pints of porter
Destroying time with vast spaces of unbroken silence
Until the evening brings its flurry of verbal blows
Aimed at no-one in particular, and everyone in general
"I'll never go back" he says
"Sure, they wouldn't have me back"
And there are thirty years in London etched
In the fleeting facial expressions
Of this elderly Connemara man who returned to find
The violently beautiful landscape of his youth destroyed
By commuter housing estates and organic cafés
"Sure, it could be worse," he says "the cow could be dead
then there'd be no milk left for the *tae*"

A mobile phone ring tone penetrates his purple ear
The eloquent voice of a rich man's wife busies itself with schedules
Orders cafe latte from behind the two-hundred year old bar
The cologne she bought in Paris unlocking a gentle smile in
    the old man's face

He shall haunt this place forever in broken shoes
Drinking pints paid for by commonage
Sold to property developers from Meath
And the children he never knew will receive
A tidy sum to buy a two bedroom duplex in Surrey
"Sure, it could be worse," he says
"The donkey could be dead
And the turf still up on the bog"

He carries his weather beaten frame
In broken shoes on an ancient cane
Down to the dimly lit pier where Connemara dips its coral finger nails
Into the Daghda's cauldron against a bastion of thrift
To the panic of seagulls and the sudden retreat of the Burren of Clare
"You'd have to carry down the turf yourself," he says
"But you could stop by the well on your way."

Her Bloody Chamber

Hands gripping, unwrapped flesh ripping
etiquette's lamb to shreds.

We tangle-limbed and helpless
receive the Eucharist of skin.

Become each others whores
blood dripping from lovers' claws

sink like canines of carnivores
into the gazelle's supple neck.

Here we feast until the last extinguished bleat
leaves us nothing to say in the stillness of our bodies

that the silence does not utter to perfection.

Son of a Goat... Part 3

Yes, okay, so I met a girl
took the black bag off my head she did
changed the record, took me by the hand
my little man-nails bitten to the quick of boyish despair
slammed the door in the face
of Mister Wall of Famished Night she did
got an apartment for us, nice place with wooden floors
stand-up lamps, too many mirrors, no stairs
and plants, wall crawlers I think.

Laid me down she did
said nice things, had clear skin
put her hand on my brow and said
everything was going to be okay.
I stared at the ceiling
waited for the plaster to crack
for the pictures to fall from the wall
for the house to cave in
I dreamt about it, howled about it
broke into convulsions of sweat in my sleep about it
I trembled for it, shivered for it
did unchristian things to my nethers for it
I willed it to happen I did, I did, I swear I did.

I heard my lady start to scream
shouted at me she did, told me to
"shut the fuck up shut the fuck up shut the fuck up"
some china smashed
ceramic tiles crashed to the floor
bust her lip the silly cow
cut my knuckles on something soft
she was asking for it, gagging for it
hid all the black bags under something by Chanel
drank all the booze, monopolized suffering

nailed it, killed it, made it hers
lay naked on our bed in tears she did
her alabaster smile cracked in two
the inside of her thighs swirling like a thunderstorm
her red eyes boiling in her skull
just then bang, hooray, the roof caved in
slap, eureka, the walls caught fire
she pleaded with me to stop she did
said that she loved me
the chancer the swindler the whore
found her out at once I did
the face was different entirely different
and the body also, beautiful, young
master of disguise she was
wore the face of a thousand women
Did she think I was stupid?
I'd know that bitch's voice anywhere
been hearing it all my life.

Then someone laughed
a woman's voice.

You know who
again I think.

The Demon

The old man with his face-pressed-flat

>   against your window his black eyes
>   watched you while you lay dreaming.

His hot hands soft against your ripe boy-flesh

>   his breath like your mothers
>   his voice like your sisters.

The wasp that crawls into your ear

>   while you are sleeping
>   the one that won't stop whispering

the darkest secrets of butterflies and men

>   the ones that shudder
>   in the rotting bark of you.

You are fucked like your parents

and your children also

are mine.

Visions of the Divine on Hare Island

Slapped back upon the heels
of a drum
        on the hunched-back heather

was a sliver of a myth-made-mad
on the March
        of a goddess of a Hun

turned up with Buddha
        with a lip-curled, red-raw gum.

Stood Pharaoh in a southpaw's stance
        with his black bride
               screaming like a wiccan
at a blind man's dance.

Sprang panic from the Sanskrit gloom
        Bad dream, mad head
               last seen, half-dead,

part birth, part messenger of unspent doom
        first spring seen
               scratching on the surface

        of a still-born moon.

Cigar in Mouth

Out of exploding warehouses, bass bins booming
1980s rock, cigar in mouth.

Out of carrion, naked, starving, chip on shoulder
still singing, closet choir boy.

Out of innocence, stealing snowflakes from
some other's Happy Christmas

Out of boyhood, in love with song; the weight
of dead generations awkward between your bullock's legs.

Out of mediocrity, still naked, still singing, caged tears
on fire for another's impossible skin.

Out of bars, flanked by jukebox princesses
and slot machine angels; keyless, hopeless, nameless, mad.

Out of loneliness and into apathy, short back and sides
nailing dreams to the chipboard to-do list.

Out of suffering not for want; hands tied up
against bare poles in love with life's bondage

Out of office or is it orifice? Bleeding for a saviour,
praying, grovelling, Pilate's last whimper in the whispering dust.

Winter, dying, love, song, landscape
the eternal tumble and the screaming salt-sea wind.

Tammy on the Footbridge

Missing two teeth
fishnets torn on turkey-thighs.

Limping in high heels
like Bambi on ice.

Stitches in her lip
a plaster on her swollen left eye.

She tells me her second child
has been taken from her

placed in a House of Bees
like the one we once shared.

Red leather skirt
hiked up to her vendor's crotch

black tears run filthy
into her broken scabbed mouth.

My hand on her cheek
Tammy in my unbreakable arms

because we understand
that addiction is not always a choice

when the hand that feeds you
is a pirate's hook.

A Letter to Prague

Scattering letters like confetti
    upon the blank page of now.

Hurling dreams like roman candles
    into the blind skies of tomorrow.

In your image a creeping metamorphosis of life unfurls

        from cocoon silk to butterfly
        from chrysalis to dragon.

Breathing fire upon the playground of my wild and swirling self

        a wind caught in the sails
        upon the galleon of my being.

Where I am rogue prince of many loves reborn in clown flesh

        torn from the bones of mischief
        man-oak stripped of foliage
        perfect science robbed of reason.

A tiger's skeleton poised to pounce frozen against your white sky

        fingers like the frail ends of branches
        shivering to the warm breeze

and the thought of you a trembling nebula of entire galaxies

        caught in a shuddering glimpse.

A letter from God in a tongue I want to understand completely

        black spaces between shimmering stars
        the answers to everything

    in a universe wrapped in your skin.

A Love Letter for The Queen of Wasps

She is murder for murder's sake.

>Withering veins and stinking flesh
>fertile soil in a nest of bones
>fire and feather in a screaming clinch
>smashed glass and new born skin
>a love song for my one true love.

She is vengeance for vanity's sake:

>A headline scrawled on toilet wall tiles
>in an underground bar in East Berlin.
>Written in hieroglyphs and signed
>sincerely in daredevil red.

Walks in with chaos in a wedding gown of shimmering white.
Down the aisle of vanishing summers and gives herself gladly
to reason in funeral black.

>A crown of thorns on a peeled blood-orange.

>>Lips that purse to kiss will bleed
>>arms ajar to hold will break
>>we both may suffer sudden lockjaw
>>with a tongue that's cocked to talk but can't.

>A halo above a clitoris.

>>365 days of every year an orgy for my
>>Valentine. Champagne and sorbet amongst
>>Saharan dunes. A rifle exploding in a sniper's
>>face. Pellet scars and poison thorns.

>The belly of the beast laid bare.

We could let the corpse of chaos rot my love. In a coffin made of each other's absence; sentenced to death by chasms left by the all too seldom intertwining fabric of our minds.

To oblivion, with a kiss,

    (for eternity has always been the space between our lips).

Techno

"Sure" said Techno
"What use has man for wind
save his own?

Can he not see as far
and as wide as the bionic eye?
To the edge of the universe;
to the heights of the limits
of his imagination.

So go figure.

For in the end
beyond the last echo
of his final transmission
we are all but flotsam and jetsam
odd old ends left to heartbreak and rust;
the broken machinery of mankind's endeavour
strewn out over time's beleaguered landscape."

Then Techno flicked off his switches
and lay down to die
amongst the neon daffodils
dreaming of electric hummingbirds.

"Personally" he concluded
"I could not give
one virtual fuck
of a digital nought
if they cover the whole world
in their machines.
For all I care
they can block out the sky
and extinguish the sun
so long as I can watch
the moon
on TV."

The Bottle in the Cupboard

There is a bottle in the cupboard but the kitchen door is locked.
It is a bottle made of green glass filled with the elixir of forced smiles;

a bottle worth more than the sum of the all the broken Christmas presents
we children opened year after year.

A bottle worth more than the sum of the joint reciprocals of our childhoods;
worth more than the sum of all my mother's makeup smeared across her face with tears.

It is a bottle that does not exist, for it is a bottle in her bedroom but the bedroom door is locked.

It is a bottle that has a song; an unscrewed cap followed by a percussive splash and finished with a gulp.

It is an aria of denial.

It is a song worth more than the sum of all the pain from all the bruises that children hide from teachers.

It is a song worth more than a child's stutter.

Worth more than the sum of a sister's innocence, squandered unwillingly to a surrogate uncle.

It is a song worth more than the sum of maternal love.

It is a song that does not sing at all

There are many bottles on the shelf where I now work twenty-five years on serving that same elixir to wise old men one of who tells me as I hand him his pint.

You might have a thousand women
But you'll only ever have one mother.

And the words that lodge in my throat are worth more than the sum of every hidden bottle behind every locked cupboard door.

For there is bottle in my childhood but the kindergarten door is locked.

It is a bottle worth more than the sum of every girl whose heart I ever broke.

Worth more than the sum of all the equal parts of absolute loneliness.

A bottle worth more than the sum of every word to the power of every time I ever heard a woman say *I love you.*

A Christmas Poem for A

No fairy lights upon skeletal branches
to punctuate the darkness with song
no children.

No midnight mass for God's first-born
in the twinkling heavens no twinkling
no God never was.

Upon the black plains of landscapes
painted in the pictures of folk half-mad with cheer
no snowman, no carrot, nothing.

And a condom atop a Christmas tree
and a suicide bomber inside a Christmas cracker
and a turkey stuffed with fibre glass.

For Tiny Tim a brand new broken leg
for Santa a brand new brand, for Christmas
a brand new ghost haunted by Christmas present.

In the festive thaw and the con
a scarf, a bobble hat, a battered wife and a screaming child
a puddle and two buttons for four blind eyes.

Jingle bells Batman smells
Robin flew away.

An Irish Thing

Oh yes for the wind that
tears the skin from your bones

save God for the tears
that shall put out your eyes

give blood to the blade
that will cut off your head

and bottle your love
for the dreams of the dead

Oh save me your skin
and gift wrap your loathing

Please watch me a while
as I crawl out of carrion

Oh yes for the crows
that shall pick at your flesh

and the God of all fire
that has hatched in a nest

lend your scream to the silence
that wets in your bed

and then bottle it all up
until the day you are dead.

Chronic Anxiety Jazz Solo No 4

Breath, you can open your eyes, soon you shall sleep. Yoda? Is that you? Ah yes, old friend and I see you have brought Ian Dury, Roxy Music and Kermit the frog.

A shepherd to guide us from the shrivelling, shrinking shadow of ourselves
on a altar made of our penance and pain, a shepherd to bring us home
and put on the Sex Pistols put the volume up full blast, smash stuff up and say
"yes my son you are man."

It rained on our sensibilities. That day when all things mattered and love was a song
that we left to be sang by worshippers who gazed towards a virtual Mecca
in the face of a nightmare written by the ghost that produced and directed your dreams
in the fuck-off finger-held-high to the sky of it all we waited, for some beating, raving, sweating thing with a hot muzzle of dribbling dirt with manners laced with kindness like speed

and empathy was the greatest E we ever took

we waited forever

for a Mohawk with a bible in the presence a policeman transvestite in fish nets
with the voice of our Father that would always roar with whips for a choir
and serrated winged words and some poor berated soul burnt at the stake

and our voice at last and at once was a ghosts

at the heart's altar

and a want and a prayer and a song

for stillness at last.

How long has it been since you pissed?

— Sir, your name Sir?

My name you would not understand, for it is in a frequency beyond your hearing.

It would peel off your skin, rape your daughter and behead your firstborn son.

— Sir there is someone else here, we are not alone here.

No, we are not

Drone's Requiem

All around, from an unfathomable distance

> the orchestras of wind played by the fingers of
> doubt build, conducted by the bare breeze-driven
> branches of trees dying in silver snapshot frames
> signed in tinsel tears on postcards to America.

Puts back on the now broken face
that has been scrubbed out
and blinks for the very last time.

> Come, it is time.

Let us at last and at once put a flame to the black page of the endless sky.

Curtains close

The stage is black.

A ghost on the piano, cracked waltz of alabaster spectres
a thrash of limbs then silence.

Who dreamt of rats and who was it who choked on a pigeon-song?

It was your mother's head bereft of skin
it was a worm in the apple your father's eye
it was a claw running through your sister's hair.

SPOTLIGHT: 4 SECONDS
A FADED PHOTOGRAPH: Fishing rods and the still lake, a beloved uncle.

Sperm-skin reborn into masculine horror
torn in binds of sinew at dawn, coronation and
a crown of thorns, all the winged choirs of cruel daylight.

ENTERS AT NOON: (LIGHTS ON): the choreographer of wasps.

A crooked smile and a man's shadow
the inventor of pig-talk choking on your name
sets fire to the photo album.

EXITS AT DUSK: (LIGHTS OFF): THE QUEEN BEE AND ALL HER DRONES.

CURTAINS CLOSE.

About the Author

STEPHEN MURRAY was born in Ireland in 1974 and moved to London in 1975. His formative years were spent living with his mother and sister in Erin Pizzey's historic shelter for battered wives in West London. As a teenager, whilst living in a children's home, he was twice a runner-up in the W.H. Smith Young Writer of the Year Awards. In 2005 he was crowned Cúirt Grand Slam Champion. He has performed his work as guest reader at many of the World's most famous poetry venues. He currently lives and writes in Galway where he works as director of Inspireland, teaching poetry and creative writing to young people across the country. *House of Bees* is his debut collection.